HR Analytics Handbook

HR Analytics Handbook

Laurie Bassi
Rob Carpenter
Dan McMurrer

Reed Business

© Reed Business, Amsterdam 2012

First edition:	November 2010
Authors:	Laurie Bassi, Rob Carpenter, Dan McMurrer
Research:	Jeroen Delmotte, Luk Smeyers
Publisher:	Reed Business, Rosa García López
Production:	Leo Schmahl
Design:	Manipal Digital Systems
Cover Design:	Ambit Creative Group

Reed Business bv, Postbus 152, 1000 AD Amsterdam.
McBassi & Company, 129 S. Eldridge Way, Golden, CO 80401, USA.

To order this book: handbook   mcbassi.com

ISBN 978-0-615-59902-1

Contents

7

Preface

HR analytics is a topic whose time has come. By bringing rigor and discipline to the "people side of the business," HR analytics helps organizations improve their performance by better aligning the management and development of people with business goals and objectives.

Over the past few years, we have seen a surge of interest among our clients in using HR analytics. This reflects both *opportunity* and *necessity*. The opportunity is a function of technological advances that have made HR analytics increasingly feasible in businesses big and small. The necessity is driven by the fact that human capital management is emerging as one of the few remaining sources of sustainable competitive advantage for an organization. Given the high stakes, decision-making by guesswork and intuition is no longer sufficient. That is precisely why we've written this handbook.

The book is designed to be an accessible, practical guide for busy HR practitioners and executives. Its focus is on making it easy for you to quickly grasp the most important aspects of HR analytics. The discussion is organized as follows:

1. What is HR analytics, why now, and how is it used?
2. How to get started, needed skills, and pitfalls to avoid
3. A summary of recent empirical findings
4. Examples of organizations using HR analytics
5. Conclusions

A synthesis of almost five years (January 2006 to October 2010) of research, analysis, and writings on HR analytics forms the book's foundation. We are grateful to our able and energetic colleagues at iNostix.com for providing us with a detailed compilation of books, referred journal articles, trade publications, and working papers that have been produced over the past decade.

We used the iNostix.com list as our starting point, and deployed a systematic process for ranking each article, report, and white paper by the extent to which it makes an original contribution to the HR analytics empirical literature. (We did not, however, use this ranking for consideration of books for inclusion.) Our ranking and selection process and criterion can be found in Appendix A. A complete list of the documents that we used in creating the summaries and insights included in this handbook can be found in Appendix B.

Although we have attempted to be thorough in our review, it is likely there are many valuable articles on specific applications of HR analytics, such as training impact or employee engagement, that have escaped our notice. So although this is not an exhaustive summary of the state of knowledge on HR analytics, it is our hope that you will find it to be clear, concise, and helpful. With that said, let's dive in!

What is HR analytics, why now, and how is it used?

1

HR analytics refers to the application of a methodology and integrated process for improving the quality of people-related decisions for the purpose of improving individual and/or organizational performance.

Although HR analytics relies on statistical tools and analysis, in its most successful form it involves much more than that. At a minimum, it requires high-quality data, leadership, broad-based agreement that analytics is a legitimate and helpful way to improve performance, well-chosen targets, and talented analysts.

As in most newly emergent disciplines, the language people use to discuss HR analytics can be confusing. Many authors, for example, choose the term "human capital analytics." Boudreau and Ramstad discuss a "talentship decision-science."[1] For the purpose of clarity and simplicity, we will treat these terms (and variations thereof) as synonymous, and will draw equally on the works of authors and researchers that use a variety of related terms.

It is also important to note that HR analytics is one component of a larger development known as "evidence-based management"[2] or "competing on analytics."[3] Here is a sampling of how some of the luminaries in this fast-developing field of management define and discuss it:

- Jac Fitz-enz: "Analytics is a mental framework, a logical progression first and a set of statistical tools second."[4]
- Wayne Cascio and John Boudreau: "Analytics is about drawing the right conclusions from data. It includes statistics and research design, and then goes beyond them to include skill in identifying and articulating key issues, gathering and using appropriate data within and outside the HR functions, setting the appropriate balance between statistical rigor and practical relevance, and building analytical competencies throughout the organization. Analytics transforms HR logic and measures into rigorous, relevant insight."[5]

- Jeffrey Pfeffer and Robert Sutton: "If taken seriously, evidence-based management can change how every manager thinks and acts. First and foremost, it is a way of seeing the world and thinking about the craft of management. Evidence-based management proceeds from the premise that using better, deeper logic and employing facts to the extent possible permits leaders to do their jobs better. Evidence-based management is based on the belief that facing the hard facts about what works and what doesn't, understanding the dangerous half-truths that constitute so much conventional wisdom about management, and rejecting the total nonsense that too often passes for sound advice will help organizations perform better."[6]
- Thomas Davenport, Jeanne Harris, and Robert Morison: "Fact-based decisions employ objective data and analysis as the primary guides to decision making. The goal of these guides is to get at the most objective answer through a rational and fair-minded process, one that is not colored by conventional wisdom or personal biases. Whenever feasible, fact-based decision makers rely on the scientific method - with hypotheses and testing - and rigorous quantitative analysis. They eschew deliberations that are primarily based on intuition, gut feeling, hearsay, or faith, although each of these may be helpful in framing or assessing a fact-based decision."[7]

WHY NOW?

Why is so much attention now being paid to HR analytics? In a nutshell, this increased attention is the result of both opportunity and necessity:
- The **opportunity** arises from the growing availability of readily accessible data on virtually every aspect of the management and development of people – data that, with some analytic ingenuity and the assistance of ever-more powerful and accessible software applications, can be transformed into valuable, actionable insights and intelligence.
- The **necessity** arises from the growing centrality of human capital management as an essential organizational core competence. "Globalization has left only one true path to profitability for firms operating in high-wage, developed nations: to base their competitive strategy on exceptional human capital management."[8] This exceptional human capital management, in turn, is not

possible without the application of HR analytics. This reality is no longer limited to firms operating in developed nations; it is increasingly true for firms in the developing world, as well.

Here is what two other authors have to say about the question of "Why now?":

- "The old HR measures, such as head count, the cost of compensation and benefits, time to fill, and turnover, no longer cut it in this new world of accountability. They don't go far enough to create shareholder value and align people decisions with corporate objectives. The effort requires putting some hard science around issues that have traditionally been thought of as difficult to quantify, like why people leave the company or how engaged they are in their jobs. When realized, human-capital metrics can provide meaningful correlations that help predict behavior and human-capital investment demands well ahead of the annual budget."[9]
- "The cost of human capital is two to six times the cost of financial capital. Rather than accepting labor only as an expense on the income statement, finance is coming to realize the cost of human capital is so great and the power of leverage that hides within it is so powerful that human capital demands a new management model."[10]

THE PURPOSE AND USES OF HR ANALYTICS

It is noteworthy that none of the preceding quotations discuss using HR analytics to "prove the value of HR." This is an issue that merits being addressed head-on. Many HR practitioners are interested in the emerging field of HR analytics as a way to prove the value of the HR function and/or its programs, or to provide justification for HR investments and headcount.

This, in our view, should not be the primary reason for doing HR analytics, as from a practical perspective, it immediately calls into question the credibility of any findings, insights, and recommendations that emerge. In short, if executives believe the HR function is embarking on an analytics project to justify itself, its budgets, or its programs, the outcomes from the project will be viewed with suspicion (even if the analysis is done well). More substantively, such a perspective fails to capitalize on the tremendous value that can be created for an organization as a whole from the effective application of HR analytics.

Indeed, "proving the value of HR" may well be a by-product of an HR analytics project. By establishing meaningful systems and methodologies for understanding and linking measures on the "people side of the business" to key performance indicators (KPIs), the potential for rigorously identifying how HR policies, procedures, systems, and interventions drive organizational performance is greatly enhanced. But it is also possible this process will reveal deficiencies in an organization's current HR strategies and programs. Hence, pursuing HR analytics takes some courage. It brings a new accountability to the HR function, which many leading-edge HR practitioners welcome. This is a critical part of earning HR's long-sought "seat at the table."

So if the purpose of HR analytics is **not** about proving the value of HR, what is its purpose? The purpose of HR analytics is simple: it is to provide insights that can be used to improve individual and organizational performance.

The uses and applications of HR analytics, however, are tremendously varied and complex. Currently, some of the most common uses include measuring and improving employee engagement, improving leadership effectiveness, and increasing sales productivity. But HR analytics has many other uses, including but not limited to improving safety, increasing the success rates of mergers and acquisitions, increasing workforce diversity, improving customer satisfaction and retention, decreasing unwanted employee turnover, and measuring the impact of culture on organizational performance.

Others have provided specific guidance on how to use analytics to address and improve a wide range of different talent-related issues. For example, in one of the most comprehensive reference documents available on the topic of HR analytics, Cascio and Boudreau[11] describe different ways of using analytics to address and improve each one of the following talent-related issues:
- Cost of absenteeism
- Cost of employee separations (turnover)
- Employee health, wellness, and welfare
- Employee attitudes and engagement

- Financial effects of work-life programs
- Staffing utility
- Economic value of job performance
- Payoff of enhanced selection
- Costs and benefits of HR development programs
- Talent-investment analysis

Similarly, the figure below identifies six major categories of uses for analytics that appear in a recent *Harvard Business Review* article, listed from "simplest to most sophisticated."[12]

Applying Talent Analytics

Six kinds of analytics can help companies answer critical talent questions—listed here from simplest to most sophisticated.

Human-Capital Facts	Human-Capital Investment Analysis	Talent Value Model
What are the key indicators of my organization's overall health? JetBlue analysts developed a metric—the "crewmember net promoter score"—that monitors employee engagement and predicts financial performance.	**Which actions have the greatest impact on my business?** By keeping track of the satisfaction levels of delivery associates, Sysco improved their retention rate from 65% to 85%, saving nearly $50 million in hiring and training costs.	**Why do employees choose to stay with—or leave—my company?** Google suspected that many of its low-performing employees were either misplaced in the organization or poorly managed. Employee performance data bore that out.
Analytical HR	**Workforce Forecasts**	**Talent Supply Chain**
Which units, departments, or individuals need attention? Managers at Lockheed Martin use an automated system to collect timely performance-review data and identify areas needing improvement.	**How do I know when to staff up or cut back?** Dow Chemical has a custom modeling tool that predicts future head count for each business unit and can adjust its predictions for industry trends, political or legal developments, and various "what if" scenarios.	**How should my workforce needs adapt to changes in the business environment?** Retail companies can use analytics to predict incoming call-center volume and release hourly employees early if it's expected to drop.

Figure 1.1 Applying talent analytics

Source: Thomas Davenport, Jeanne Harris, and Jeremy Shapiro, "Competing on Talent Analytics," *Harvard Business Review*, October 2010, p. 4.

In summary, the purpose of HR analytics is to improve performance. Its uses and applications are very broad-based, touching on any and all aspects of individual and organizational human capabilities (or deficiencies) affecting key organizational outcomes.

How to get started, needed skills, and common pitfalls to avoid

2

As noted above, the specifics of HR analytics can vary widely, based on organization, industry, issue to be addressed, and dozens of other factors. However, it is possible to outline some general principles for getting started and avoiding the most common hazards. This section addresses those topics.

While HR analytics comes in many forms, we focus most of our discussion below on the most difficult – and most strategic – application of HR analytics: linking people-related measures to key organizational business results. We do this primarily because the lessons from applying HR analytics in this realm are also broadly applicable to other uses of HR analytics as well, and because most organizations are still striving to develop the capacity to apply HR analytics strategically. For readers interested in additional details on the "how-to's" of HR analytics, the end of the section provides a number of suggestions for additional reading on the implementation of HR analytics, all the way from the simplest application to the most complex.

IDENTIFYING STAKEHOLDERS AND THEIR REQUIREMENTS

The first step in a well-designed HR analytics process is to identify the key stakeholders and their requirements: what they need to know to improve individual and organizational performance. Stakeholders can range all the way from front-line managers, to the heads of major divisions, functions, or business units, to the CEO and chair of the board of directors. Each of these stakeholders will have a different, but related, set of concerns; they will want to know how people-related data can be used and analyzed in order to help them achieve the results for which they have responsibility.

The "higher" the stakeholder sits in an organization and the greater their span of influence/responsibility, the broader and more strategic will be the nature of their concerns. So, for example, a front-line manager might be concerned with the high rate of employee turnover in a particular job function or geographic location, and what might be done to reduce it. The CFO, on the other hand, might be focused on broader questions like rapidly increasing health care costs and what might be done to slow down or reverse this increase. The CEO will want to know the answers to even more far-reaching questions: what can be done on the people side of the business to grow revenues, contain costs, and increase profitability.

HR ANALYTICS IN CONTEXT

As a general rule, the broader and more strategic an issue, the more challenging (and more important) it is to address through the application of solid HR analytics. Benchmarking and scorecards certainly have their place and can provide great value in limited contexts. But there is much greater potential impact in HR analytics projects that are based on valid and rigorous measurement and designed to identify causal relationships and leading (rather than lagging) indicators of organizational performance (see figure below for a graphical depiction of the different levels of value from various forms of HR measurement and reporting).

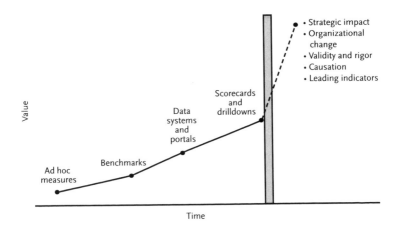

Figure 2.1 Hitting the wall in HR measurement

Source: John Boudreau and Peter Ramstad, *Beyond HR: The New Science of Human Capital,* Harvard Business Press (2007), p. 189.

In most cases, it is valuable to view HR analytics within the perspective of an ongoing cycle (see graphic below). Falletta writes, "To effectively build robust HR intelligence [analytics] capabilities that are both proactive and systematic, HR intelligence [analytics] must be positioned as an ongoing cycle involving the following critical steps:

1. Determining stakeholder requirements,
2. Defining the HR research agenda,
3. Identifying data and information sources,
4. Gathering data and information,
5. Transforming data and information,
6. Communicating and using intelligence results, and
7. Enabling strategy creation, decision-making, execution and learning."[13]

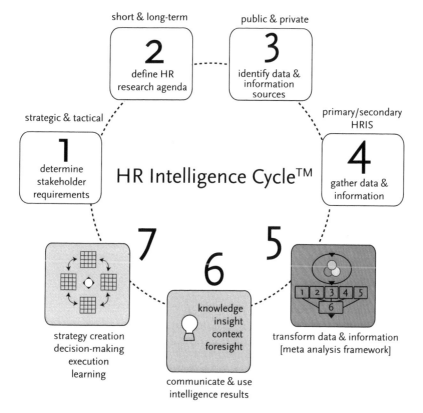

Figure 2.2 HR intelligence cycle

Source: Salvatore Falletta, "HR Intelligence: Advancing People Research and Analytics" by Leadersphere, *IHRIM Journal* 2008 – vol. XII, no. 3, p. 24.

One of the significant benefits that can result from incorporating HR analytics into this type of ongoing cycle is that it provides an authentic and meaningful way for HR practitioners to be involved with key stakeholders throughout their organization, working collaboratively to help improve the outcomes that are most critical to them.

A FIRST STEP: LEARNING TO THINK ABOUT "NATURALLY-OCCURRING EXPERIMENTS"

For the most strategic types of HR analytics projects – those linking measures on the people side of the business to organizational results – it is often helpful to think about "naturally occurring experiments" within an organization. Even though the organization may be governed by a single set of HR policies and procedures, there is usually remarkable variation in how well and effectively these policies and procedures are implemented.

This variation generates a naturally occurring experiment (e.g., think of an organization with 30 different sales offices, all selling the same products, but with very different rates of success). The variation in success rates provides a potential goldmine for learning about the human drivers (or impediments) of organizational results. It can provide an answer to executives who view the results and ask the logical question, "Why are some of our sales teams more effective than others?"

In other contexts, the questions might be "Why do we have much higher rates of employee turnover among some call center teams than we do among others?" or "Why are some managers able to attract and retain a highly diverse workforce, while others are not?" There is no end to these "why" questions (or the stakeholders who want answers to them). They exist for every aspect of the business that is touched by human behavior – that is, every aspect of the business.

By collecting the right data and analyzing it in the right way, it is entirely possible to capitalize on the natural experiments and answer these questions. (Multiple such examples of actual applications of HR analytics are described in later sections of this handbook.) The insights resulting from the analysis can then be used to foster fact-based decision-making in service of improved organizational performance. That is the essence of HR analytics.

Alternatively, some people find it helpful to think in "Six Sigma" terms. Six Sigma began as a set of analytic practices targeted at improving processes and eliminating defects (undesirable outcomes) in manufacturing, but its principles can be applied in a variety of other business contexts. The insight here is similar to that which comes from viewing an organization as a naturally occurring experiment: there are negative (and positive) sources of variance responsible for defective (good) results, and it is possible to deploy analytic techniques to identify these sources of variance – in this case, the people-related sources. Knowing the sources of variation in results is the key to laying the foundation for an evidence-based approach to decision-making.

QUESTIONS TO BE ANSWERED

Its ability to link people to results makes HR analytics a powerful tool to help answer a variety of critical business questions. Before that can be done, however, there are a number of challenges that must be addressed during the course of this work, including the following:

- Identifying key performance indicators
- Determining the best possible analytic methods to apply to the project
- Effectively communicating the results
- Building a follow-through strategy

IDENTIFYING KEY PERFORMANCE INDICATORS

One of the first discoveries many HR practitioners make when they embark on an HR analytics project is that it requires them to become immersed in and knowledgeable about the operations and finances of their organization. Linking measures on the "people side of the business" to key performance indicators requires knowing what the KPIs of the organization are. And, of course, KPIs will vary across lines of business and levels of management. Front-line managers will have more tactical responsibilities and that will be reflected in their KPIs, whereas senior executives will have more strategic KPIs as their responsibilities. Some organizations will have relatively few KPIs, but other organizations may literally have hundreds of KPIs.

Sorting through all this can be challenging. In identifying the best KPIs for any given HR analytics project, one should seek to identify KPIs with the following characteristics:

1. *Most important to the stakeholder*
   Although leaders and managers may have many KPIs for which they have responsibility, there are always a small handful that are the most critical (the ones that "keep them awake at night"). These are the KPIs on which to focus.

2. *Available on a timely basis*
   In order to link metrics on the people side of the business to these KPIs, it is necessary that the KPIs be available without long delays. So, for example, a KPI that is only available 12 months after the fact will have limited use in helping to understand the *current* linkages between people and results.

3. *A significant level of potential data disaggregation (or "granularity")*
   In order to link variations in people measures to variations in the KPIs, it is necessary to be able to actually observe variation. Hence, a very high-level KPI (such as a firm's stock price) does not provide a solid foundation for doing HR analytics work (at least within any individual firm), because at any point in time, the firm only has a single stock price. But a KPI available at a more granular (disaggregated) level, such as performance of sales teams, provides a much better basis for doing HR analytics work.

DETERMINING THE BEST POSSIBLE ANALYTIC METHODS

Selection of analytic methods is primarily a function of the number of data points ("observations," such as the number of sales offices that can be compared) available for analysis, and secondarily the time period(s) for which data are available. In general, the greater the number of observations, the more sophisticated the analytic methods that become possible. The number of data points available will, in turn, be determined by the appropriate "unit of analysis" for the KPI under consideration.

So, for example, when the KPI of interest can be measured at the level of the individual employee (such as employee engagement), many observations will be available, making possible the use of more sophisticated multivariate statistical techniques (e.g., regression or factor analysis). But when the KPI of interest can only be measured at a much more aggregated level (e.g., safety outcomes at the plant level), there are many fewer observations, necessitating the use of simpler statistical techniques (such as t-test or correlations). Should "panel data" (a time-series on a cross-section of data) be available for analysis, then "panel estimation techniques," among the most sophisticated methodologies available for HR analytics, can be employed. While a more detailed exploration of these methods is beyond the scope of this handbook, there are many excellent guides available on the subject of how to apply the appropriate statistical analysis techniques to available data.

EFFECTIVELY COMMUNICATING RESULTS

A critical factor determining the success of an HR analytics project is how effectively the findings and insights are communicated back to the stakeholders. Regardless of the sophistication and complexity of the analysis itself, the results need to be simple, clear, and actionable when presented to stakeholders.

In general, the analysis should be presented in summary form (avoiding a "data dump"), with additional details provided in an appendix or reference document (for those readers who are interested in understanding exactly how the analysis was done). Finding visual ways to present the findings is vital in making complex information easy for stakeholders to understand. Additional insights into how to interpret the findings as well as recommendations for what actions are suggested by the results should also be incorporated. Stakeholders will look to the presenter as the expert and will typically welcome efforts to make the implications of the analysis clear and relevant.

BUILDING A FOLLOW-THROUGH STRATEGY

In most organizations, taking a rigorous, fact-based approach to decision-making about the people side of the business will represent a new way of doing things. Some managers and executives will understand it quickly, and embrace it. Others will come along more slowly. Therefore, a follow-through strategy is necessary, including periodically touching base with stakeholders to see how they are using the findings and insights, and what can be done to help them make more effective use of the analysis. Finding ways to celebrate the success of "early adopters" can help to get the word out to the rest of the organization, so they can better understand the potential benefits they might realize through the use of HR analytics.

Ultimately, HR analytics should be embedded in business processes and an organization's performance management system. When an organization has arrived at a point where HR analytics is being used to guide major investment and strategic choices, it will be able to have a significant, positive, and ongoing impact on the organization.

THE SKILLS NEEDED TO BE SUCCESSFUL

This section draws heavily on the best discussion we have found on the individual and organizational skills necessary for analytics to achieve its full potential within an organization: *Analytics at Work*, authored by Thomas Davenport, Jeanne Harris and Robert Morison.[14] The authors note:

> Though computers and data drive analytical decision making, they are not nearly as vital as people: we've never seen an analytically oriented firm without plenty of analytically oriented people. Finding, developing, managing, and deploying analysts – the people who make the day-to-day work of such organizations possible – is critical to a firm's success.[15]

They go on to observe that effective analysts need to be proficient not only with data, but also with people, incorporating all of the following skill sets: [16]
- Quantitative and technical
- Business knowledge and design
- Relationship and consulting
- Coaching and staff development

They define four types of analytical people within an organization:
1. Analytical champions: "executive decision makers who depend heavily on data analyses to make business decisions and who lead major analytical initiatives."[17]

2. Analytical professionals: "the most proficient and knowledgeable employees across the range of quantitative skills."[18]
3. Analytical semiprofessionals: "apply the models and algorithms developed by professionals on behalf of the rest of the business."[19]
4. Analytical amateurs: "employees whose primary job is not analytical work, but who need some understanding of analytics to do their jobs successfully."[20]

The figure below summarizes the typical skill proficiency levels required for each of the four analyst types:

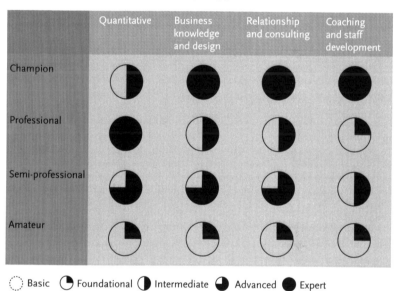

Figure 2.3 Typical skill proficiency level by type of analyst

Source: Jeanne G. Harris, Elizabeth Craig and Henry Egan, "How to Create a Talent-Powered Analytical Organization," Accenture Institute for High Performance research report, November 2009, p. 6.

Having the right type of analytical people, with the right types of quantitative, business, relationship, consulting, and coaching skills is absolutely necessary - but is not sufficient in and of itself. Analytics needs to be embedded in business processes and built into an organization's culture. Davenport, et al. observe, "Whenever we go to a company that is really good at analytics, we find that an analytical orientation is deeply embedded into its culture. The principles of an analytical culture go beyond the particular attitudes of individual decision makers, and they're rarely communicated as lists of precepts; they're usually things that people just know."[21]

These are, no doubt, daunting requirements for HR practitioners just getting started on HR analytics (or who work in organizations that lack an "analytics culture.") *Analytics at Work* provides guidance for practitioners and executives seeking to develop more analytic capability within their organizations. Specific advice is provided on how to move all the way from stage 1 ("analytically impaired") to stage 2 ("localized analytics") to stage 3 ("analytical aspirations") to stage 4 ("analytical companies") to stage 5 ("analytical competitors").

The HR department itself is an excellent place to get started in this transition, by starting to hire, develop, and reward analytical people. It is always important to remember, however, that HR analytics, "is not just an HR exercise – it requires the collaboration of IT, HR, and the business to bring together the tools and information with the expertise to use that information in meaningful ways."[22]

THE ROLE OF TECHNOLOGY

In recent years, technology tools have played an increasingly important role in enhancing organizations' capacity to apply HR analytics in a useful, insightful way. There are numerous categories of software and other technology applications (often collectively called "HR technologies") that facilitate the collection, storage, and processing of data necessary for HR analytics to be successful.

These applications fall into the broad categories of HR administration, service delivery, workforce management, talent management, and business intelligence,[23] and can include tools for talent acquisition, succession planning, learning management, career development, and the implementation, execution, and tracking of other people-related functions within the organization. In recent years, software that directly supports HR analytic techniques has become more common. Section 3 (below) explores the impact that the use of such applications has had on key organizational outcomes.

Although a full exploration of the specifics of HR technologies is beyond the scope of this handbook, we would point readers to CedarCrestone's annual *HR Systems Survey* as a comprehensive source of information on their deployment and use.[24]

COMMON PITFALLS TO AVOID

There are numerous hazards along the path to successfully using and embedding HR analytics in an organization. A number are described frequently throughout the literature on HR analytics. The following represent some of the more common or dangerous traps, along with various authors' perspectives on why they should be avoided:

1. *Measuring what is easy versus what is important*
   HR departments often have enormous amounts of data on the HR function itself, spending considerable time and effort on HR scorecards that focus on the department's own efficiency. A recent Conference Board publication notes, "While the scorecard approach serves as a valuable means of determining *how* to use human capital metrics, it doesn't provide the more important insight into *why* metrics are important, *which* metrics to choose, or *what* they represent in terms of how human capital generates value."[25] An important step is to identify what needs to be known or measured, not necessarily what already is.

2. *Confusing benchmarking with HR analytics*
   "Benchmarking is...simply a tool for measuring the efficiencies of particular HR functions."[26] In and of itself, benchmarking does not produce actionable insights for improving individual or organizational performance.

3. *Accepting one-size-fits all solutions*
   A closely related pitfall is accepting "one-size-fits all solutions" as an alternative for doing the customized analysis required to identify the unique human drivers of an organization's business results. This is a particularly common mistake when it comes to understanding employee engagement, where careful analysis "reveals that the drivers of employee engagement across

different organizations are consistently more different than they are similar – even among businesses that are within the same industry."[27]

4. *Focusing on ROI as the "holy grail"*
"Understanding the returns and investments in HR programs and practices is useful, but the quest for ROI will not provide the entire solution to the need for a decision science…Most ROI calculations fail to change decisions about the vital human capital and organization resources. They are used primarily to demonstrate the value of HR investments after the fact. ROI creates the wrong focus."[28]

5. *Allowing perfect to be the enemy of good*
Sometimes the perfect information simply is not available, but HR professionals should not use this as an excuse; they should seek to learn from any evidence that does exist. For example, "a common criticism of some human capital indicators is that they merely record correlations, not proof of cause-and-effect relationships… While this is a valuable health warning, it is not an adequate response on its own. Managers must study such correlations, as they can provide a valuable starting point for understanding the drivers of value… while it is dangerous to over-interpret correlations, it is a missed opportunity to disregard them."[29]

6. *Seeing HR analytics as the sole province of the HR function*
"By definition, because it concerns assessment of the interaction between HR investments and the rest of the business, human capital analysis is a multidisciplinary activity, and should not be seen as one that is solely the responsibility of the HR function."[30]

GETTING STARTED: RECOMMENDED READING

There are many books that provide valuable guidance on how to get started on (or advance) HR analytics within an organization. While a complete list of sources is available at the back of the handbook in Appendix B, there are a few books that are especially noteworthy in this regard, including the following:
- *Investing in People* (Cascio and Boudreau) provides detailed guidance for undertaking a wide variety of HR analytics calculations.

- *The Business of Learning* (Vance) provides detailed guidance on how to apply analytics and the logic of economics to all aspects of the training and development function.
- *The New HR Analytics* (Fitz-enz) provides "how to" essays, case studies, and sample worksheets.
- *Analytics at Work* (Davenport et al.) provides broad-based guidance on how to create a more analytically-oriented culture within an organization.

A summary of recent empirical findings

3

USE OF HR ANALYTICS

Davenport et al. conclude, "Companies that want to compete on talent analytics must have access to high-quality data and manage them at an enterprise level, support analytical leaders, choose realistic targets for analysis, and hire analysts with a broad base of expertise."[31] How many organizations are tackling these challenges, why have they chosen to do so, and how well are they meeting these challenges? Much of the information about this currently comes from a variety of surveys in which organizations self-report their success in this domain.

What specific factors are driving organizations to turn to HR analytics? Analyzing 2009 survey results from 233 companies [more than two-thirds of which are actively using human capital management (HCM) "reporting or analytics, or are currently integrating those capabilities"[32]], Lombardi and White found that the two factors most prominently driving the use of analytics were an organization's need to adapt to the changing business climate and cost issues forcing more rigor around HCM decisions.[33] Each factor was cited by almost half of survey respondents.

Based on a survey of over 400 North American HR professionals, IBM/Cognos found that there was significant consensus on the major benefits of workforce analytics, with 76 percent citing improvements in workforce management, 69 percent citing improved levels of workforce productivity, and 67 percent mentioning greater return on investments in talent management[34] (see graphic below). Based on additional survey results (discussed below), however, it is clear that many organizations pursuing HR analytics have not realized many of these potential benefits, at least not as of yet.

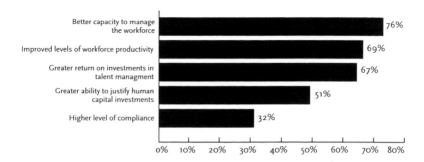

Figure 3.1 Potential benefits of workforce analytics
Source: IBM Corporation, "Getting Smart About Your Workforce: Why Analytics Matter," 2009, p. 18.

CedarCrestone's most recent annual report on organizations' use of various HR systems is based on a survey of approximately 1,000 respondents (74 percent of whom are in the HR field).[35] It finds business intelligence/workforce metrics is one of the three initiatives to which the most time is being devoted by survey respondents (along with business process improvements/innovations and talent management processes). Among all respondents, 19 percent have workforce analytics applications "in use," with an additional 20 percent budgeted for implementation in the next 12 to 36 months.

Are analytic methods being used effectively?
Another line of research has examined the extent to which organizations using HR analytics are doing so in a way that maximizes its impact within the organization.

The IBM/Cognos survey found that the 33 percent of respondents with a formal workforce analytics application in place also reported that they were more effective in five different areas than those without an analytics application: (a) developing training strategies, (b) determining strategies for reduction in force, redeployment, and retraining, (c) understanding collaboration and knowledge sharing, (d) retaining valued talent within the organization, and (e) evaluating workforce performance.[36]

They also found, however, that even among organizations using workforce analytics techniques, most are using them for purposes of identifying *historical* trends and patterns. Few are applying them, for example, to the creation of data-based future scenarios. While 36 percent of the organizations using workforce analytics identify historical patterns and trends in evaluating workforce performance, only 8 percent develop scenarios and predict future outcomes in the area of workforce performance. Similarly, 30 percent track historical trends in retaining valued talent, but only 9 percent predict future outcomes. The authors conclude that the application of "more advance analytic techniques to understand the composition and capabilities of workforces is still very much in its infancy."[37]

Gates examines a survey of 104 HC executives and finds that 71 percent of organizations report having some form of HC measures in place, but that only a small percentage of those (7 percent of all organizations) have metrics that capture information on efficiency, effectiveness, and impact (on business process and strategic outcomes).[38] Similarly, Luketic reports on a survey of 307 HR professionals and finds that 79 percent of organizations are using some form of HC metrics, with 11 percent already "strategically focused," with measures aligned to the organization's strategy.[39] Fifty-four percent, however, report that they are either in the planning/development stage or the early stage, with measures that exist but are not necessarily aligned with the business.

Magau and Roodt conducted an extensive analysis of 202 survey responses from HR professionals and line mangers inside a South African mining company.[40] They sought to determine whether there are statistically significant differences in their views on the effectiveness, efficiency, and impact of human capital on three key strategic objectives: (a) operational excellence, (b) growing the company, and (c) securing the company's future.

They found a statistically significant difference in views between the two groups on all three outcomes. The HR practitioners believed that human capital interventions added significantly more business value than line managers, who believed the interventions were much less connected to the strategic objectives. The authors concluded that line managers were "not satisfied with the current human capital solutions provided by HR management" and that human capital was therefore "not being used optimally" in the organization.[41]

Gates reports similar findings. Of the HC executives surveyed, 75 percent said that they recommended measures to managers as a way to meet key performance indicators (KPIs), but only 15 percent of those reported that business managers then used the metric for that purpose to a "significant" or "total" extent.[42]

He also finds that approximately 60 percent of organizations use measures of human capital in managers' bonus plans and in setting their MBOs (management by objectives). However, of those organizations using human capital measures in those areas, almost two-thirds stated the human capital measures align "moderately or less than moderately" or "not at all or slightly" with the organization's business targets. Gates concludes that "this lack of alignment does not bode well for the role of HCM in helping managers achieve their strategic business goals or KPIs. Such imprecision can lead to dissatisfaction with the measures used and result in poor manager evaluations of the HCM program."[43]

Data from IBM/Cognos help to shed some light on broad ways to bridge the gap between what HR knows and how it can be applied by managers elsewhere in the organization.[44] Their survey found that in organizations that report that HR "proactively contributes to strategy," 48 percent of non-HR senior executives use workforce analytics data (when available), compared with only 29 percent of non-HR senior executives in all other organizations.

Similarly, Whiteley assessed the results of a survey of over 100 business and HR leaders and found only 12 percent of respondents reported that they could identify returns on human capital investments.[45] However, among respondents reporting HR plays a "strategic" role in the organization, 50 percent describe themselves as being able to identify returns on human capital investment (compared with just 2 percent in organizations that view the HR function as being largely administrative). The survey also found a significant gap between "actual" and "desired" level of HR's HCM capability and the function's effectiveness in contributing to strategic objectives, such as linking people with performance, talent planning, and informing the organization's business strategy.

Gates also finds the most frequently-used measures of human capital are **not** the ones most respondents believe best predict outcomes (i.e., "leading" metrics).[46] Of the five measures that respondents are most likely to believe are leading metrics (employee engagement, leadership, employee commitment, readiness level, and voluntary turnover), only two are among the metrics that are most frequently tracked (employee engagement and voluntary turnover). The other three most frequently-tracked items (diversity, average age, employee satisfaction) are not among those believed to be most predictive.

Trends in use of HR analytics

There is a variety of good information on trends in HR analytics, and almost without exception, it points to increases in almost every measure: use of HR analytics, time spent, and amount budgeted. The use of more sophisticated HR analytics methods has increased, as has the strategic application of HR analytics. For more detailed information on HR analytics trends, recent CedarCrestone reports are valuable sources.[47]

Summing up

Overall, the existing information on how analytic methods are being used suggests that many organizations are beginning to deploy analytics (and that the number of such organizations continues to grow), but that there is still a long way to go for many in terms of aligning metrics with business results and achieving "buy-in" from managers. In the end, however, the organizations that already surmounted those hurdles and are most advanced in their use of HR analytics are also the ones that report realizing the greatest benefits, as discussed in the following section.

LINKING TO BUSINESS RESULTS

What links exist between HR analytics and organizations' business results? The evidence on this question falls into two (related) categories: how the use of HR analytics itself affects business results, and how various specific measures of people or human capital management are associated with business results. Evidence on the first question again comes primarily from surveys about the use of HR analytics. The sources of answers on the second question are more varied, with some coming from publicly-reported results within a single company, and others coming from cross-organizational empirical studies.[48]

Before reviewing the results in these two categories, it is important to note that many studies showing *correlations* do not establish a direct, causal link between the two. In fact, a 2005 review of 68 studies on the relationship between HR practices and firm performance suggested that in some cases, there may be "reverse causality" – firm performance preceding the improved HR practices.[49] The authors noted "high performing organizations by their nature possess slack resources... Firms that are profitable may share these profits with employees in a number of ways."[50] Having said that, it is important to remember that even correlations provide key insights into associations between variables and as such should not be ignored, merely interpreted cautiously, with the underlying relationships subject to additional analysis.

Relationship between use of HR analytics and business results

Among the organizations using HCM reporting or analytics in some way, Lombardi and White found key differences in organizational performance between those that are most mature in their application of HR applications (based on timeliness of data access, accuracy of data, and ability to use data for workforce planning) and others.[51] The most mature 20 percent (which they call "best-in-class") report 11 percent year-over-year increases in profit per employee and 6 percent year-over-year increases in revenue per employee (measured as full-time equivalents, or FTEs). The least mature 30 percent ("laggards"), on the other hand, reported a 7 percent year-over-year decline in profit per employee, and a 1 percent increase in revenue per employee.

Differences are even more dramatic in comparing organizations using HCM reporting and analytics (regardless of level of maturity) versus those that are not. Organizations using HCM reporting and analytics in some way reported a 4 percent overall year-over-year increase in profit per FTE, and a 4 percent overall increase in revenue per FTE. Those not using reporting and analytics reported declines in both measures (5 percent decline in profit per FTE, 1 percent decline in revenue per FTE). (See graphic below.)

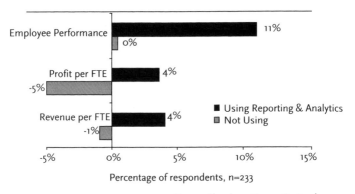

Percentage of respondents, n=233

Source: Aberdeen Group, September 2009

Figure 3.2 Year-over-year impact from use of reporting/analytics

Source: Aberdeen Group, "Human Capital Management; Workforce Analytics Drives Profit and Performance," September 2009, p. 9.

Survey results from CedarCrestone are consistent with Lombardi and White, and include the finding that organizations using workforce analytics reported 18 percent higher sales per employee.[52] The CedarCrestone report concludes with the recommendation that one of the two HR technologies with the highest business impact is a cluster of business intelligence tools that includes human capital management analytics (as well as other data and reporting technologies).[53]

The report contains multiple data comparisons showing links between the adoption of various HR technologies and better measures of sales results. For example, the report compares two-year sales growth between firms using or not using specific types of talent management applications. (To cite one example, they find sales growth of 13.9 percent among those organizations using a competency management application, compared to 8.5 percent among other organizations.) Of the seven specific applications they analyze, sales growth results are higher for organizations using the specified application in six of the cases. (See figure below.)

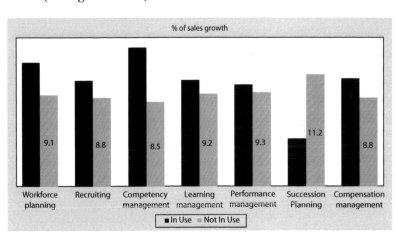

Figure 3.3 Two-year sales growth by talent management application
Source: CedarCrestone, "2009-2010 HR Systems Survey, 12th Annual Edition," p. 18.

They also find higher rates of sales growth among organizations with broader scope to their succession planning process (11.5 percent for those applying it to all managers, compared with 4.5 percent for those applying it only to top management). Organizations with talent processes and systems classified as "integrated" had two-year sales growth of 18.2 percent, compared with 9.6 percent for those with no talent management processes or systems.

Consistent findings also come from an Infohrm survey of more than 200 HR executives around the world, as reported in Roberts.[54] Roberts notes that "leading-edge" organizations (those able to "analytically identify the workforce drivers of business success; readily translate workforce analysis and findings into action; and employ an analytics Center of Excellence model with a dedicated workforce analytics team"[55]) are dramatically more likely to report that the use of analytics has influenced cost-saving decisions (63 percent of leading-edge organizations, compared to 32 percent of others) and that analytics has influenced revenue-increasing decisions (53 percent versus 14 percent).

Relationship between specific human capital measures and business results

The discussion that follows is based on a different, but related, body of research. These examples typically *apply* HR analytics in order to evaluate the impact of a wide variety of specific HCM practices on business results (in order to determine how best to improve those results), whereas the research literature discussed above focused on evaluating the impact of HR analytics *itself* (and/or the impact of HR technologies). The specific HCM practices being examined often vary from study to study, but all generally represent measures of different aspects of an organization's management and development of its employees.

Plant operations and safety   Using self-reported information (from 45 plants in the chemical manufacturing and oil/gas industries) on organizational outcomes and "maturity" levels on various HCM practices, Bassi and McMurrer found strong relationships between multiple elements of HCM and contemporaneous business results.[56] The plants reported on seven business outcomes: profitability, productivity, asset utilization, ability to attract employees, ability to retain key employees, customer satisfaction, and process safety. Each was reported relative to competitors or to "world class" standards, depending on the measure. The study used correlations and comparisons of means to identify the links between HCM and business results.

Combining the seven business outcomes, the study found five categories of HCM were the most powerful correlates of results: hiring decisions, innovation, collaboration/teamwork, accountability, and job design. Key drivers of the separate business outcomes were also identified. For example, the three most important HCM factors driving plant "process safety" were levels of maturity in the plants' knowledge accessibility systems, hiring decisions, and training. (See figure below.)

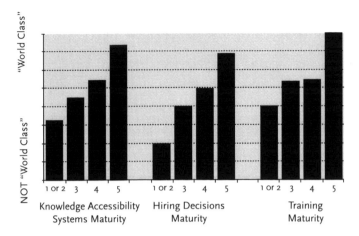

Figure 3.4 Plants' process safety status, by maturity scores on HCM items (1 = Low, 5 = High)

Source: Laurie Bassi and Daniel McMurrer, "Process Safety & People: Searching for the Human Capital Drivers of Process Safety," www.plantsuccess.com, p.6.

At American Standard (now Trane), measures of human capital "maturity" in manufacturing plants were an important predictor of plants' safety rates in the following year.[57] Plants in the top half of the distribution of human capital scores had an average safety "incident rate" that was 14 percent lower (i.e., fewer accidents) than those in the bottom half of the human capital distribution.

Changes in human capital maturity were also associated with better safety results at American Standard. Manufacturing plants with above-median increases in 5 of 5 human capital maturity categories subsequently had lower accident rates than plants with below-median changes.[58]

Financial performance At American Standard, Bassi notes, measures of human capital maturity in company sales offices are associated with higher financial success scores in the following year.[59] Financial success scores in offices in the top half of the distribution of human capital maturity were approximately 65 percent higher than those in the bottom half of the distribution. *Changes* in human capital maturity are also associated with better sales results at American Standard. Bassi and McMurrer report that sales offices with above-median increases in 4 of 5 human capital categories (all except employee engagement) had larger increases in sales income over the same time period.[60]

As noted above, human capital maturity was also associated with better safety outcomes in American Standard's manufacturing plants. Three specific human capital practices were identified as important predictors of *both* financial success and safety: (a) having employees engage in one-on-one discussions with their managers to review performance; (b) setting aside time for sharing of tips and best practices; and (c) offering training to employees that is seen as practical and applicable to day-to-day work.

Cantrell, et al. explore the effect of specific human capital processes and other factors across multiple organizations.[61] They found that organizations focusing on processes devoted to three broad areas: "creating a people strategy aligned with the business strategy, providing supportive work environments, and developing employees by giving them ample opportunity to learn and grow"[62] achieved greater economic success than those organizations focusing less on those areas (see graphic below). They find that improving by one quartile in these processes is associated with a 10 to 15 percent increase in "capital efficiency" (ratio of total annual sales to invested operational capital).

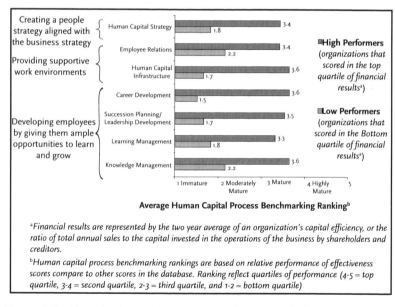

Figure 3.5 Organizations with more mature human capital processes have superior financial performance
Source: Susan Cantrell, James M. Benton, Terry Laudal, Robert J. Thomas, "Measuring the value of human capital investments: the SAP case," *Strategy & Leadership*, Emerald Group Publishing Limited: Vol. 34, No. 2 (2006), p. 50.

Marriott Vacation Club, which makes careful use of HR analytics (see additional description in section 4), found sales executive engagement was associated with significant differences in employee performance on two key company business metrics: sales volume per guest and percentage of tours closing on time-share contracts (see graphic below).[63]

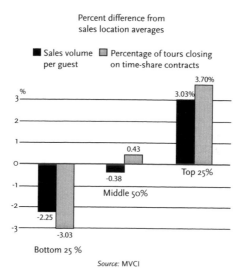

Percent difference from
sales location averages

Figure 3.6 Most engaged sales executives are more productive

Source: Stephen Gates, "Strategic Human Capital Measures; Orientation, Accountability, and Communication," The Conference Board, 2008, Research Report R – 1417-08-WG, p. 26.

Educational Outcomes Assessing results from a public school district in South Carolina, Bassi and McMurrer reported schools with higher human capital management scores (as observed by teachers and staff) had larger improvements in mean math scores on standardized tests.[64] On the other hand, Bassi and McMurrer found no links between human capital measures and learner outcomes at five "further education" colleges in the United Kingdom, although they do find significant links with employee commitment among employees of those colleges.[65]

Other Feather cites multiple examples from her organization's clients and their application of HR analytics to link people to business results.[66] Across all Fortune 500 clients, she found that companies in the lowest quartile in company profits had 50 percent fewer engaged employees than companies in the top quartile. Discussing specific (but anonymous) company examples, Feather reports the higher levels of engagement drove higher sales at a global brewery, higher volume of calls at a call center, and improved customer perceptions at a regional bank.

Bassi and McMurrer gathered HCM data on 11 publicly-traded financial services firms and examined their stock returns in the subsequent year (see graphic below).[67] Higher HCM scores were associated with higher stock returns. In a different study, the same authors found a relationship between superior human capital management and better-than-average stock returns the following year (from 2002-2010), based on portfolios of publicly-traded companies (including, but not limited to, financial services firms).[68]

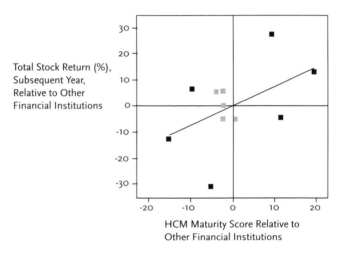

Figure 3.7 Higher HCM scores associated with better subsequent stock performance
Source: Laurie Bassi and Daniel McMurrer, "Maximizing Your Return on People," *Harvard Business Review*, 2007, Reprint R07034 p. 6.

Differences across organizations While the majority of the research cited above finds strong links between various measures of human capital and organizational performance, it is also notable to observe across the different studies the variety of specific human capital factors associated with better organizational results (in those cases that identify specific drivers).

Bassi and McMurrer directly examine the question of how similar (or different) are the drivers of business results within different organizations.[69] They measure a standard set of 69 specific human capital factors across three different organizations and, using analytic techniques to link the factors to business outcomes, conclude, "The exact list of [human capital] items most closely related to key outcomes in any given organization bears little relation to the list of most important [human capital] items in other organizations."[70]

In the end, this points back to a key lesson from the empirical findings cited above for organizations seeking to apply HR analytics techniques to address current business questions, problems, or issues. They should do so in a way that is highly customized to address the unique outcomes and unique qualities (culture, current stage of growth, etc.) of that organization specifically, and should first consider a broad range of potential human capital drivers of business results, using analytics to narrow the scope to those human capital factors found to be most important for that organization.

More broadly, the empirical studies suggest there is a strong, consistent relationship between human capital and organizational outcomes. Applying HR analytics – developing and then using the necessary data, techniques, and tools – to discern the specific nature of the relationship within an organization is now within reach for all. The following section includes a variety of short examples of organizations across multiple industries and spheres that have already begun to reap the rewards of this process.

Examples of organizations using HR analytics

4

The ways that human capital analytics can be used are as varied as the organizations using them. Some specific examples have begun to appear in the literature and there are no doubt many additional companies pursuing similar strategies that have not been publicly reported. (See table below.) Best Buy meticulously tracks employee engagement, Sysco employs analytics to find the best way to motivate its drivers, and the Beaufort County School District applies analytics to bolster student achievement.

These and other examples (often based on short "case studies" or other brief descriptions of how companies are employing the

Organization	Outcome Area Targeted
AC Milan	Trends/other
American Standard Company	Sales
Beaufort County School District	Trends/other
Best Buy	Engagement
Corestar	Sales
Engineering Limited	Leadership
Enterprise Rent-A-Car	Trends/other
Harrah's Entertainment	Engagement
Ingram Content Group	Retention
Marriott Vacation Club	Engagement
Oakland A's	Trends/other
RAC	Absenteeism
Royal Bank of Scotland	Trends/other
SAP America, Inc.	Leadership
Standard Chartered Bank	Engagement
Sysco	Incentives
United Health Group	Trends/other
Wawa	Retention

Figure 4.1 Organizations using HR analytics, and major outcome area targeted

techniques described in this handbook) are described below. They provide some flavor of the "real world" applications of analytics to organizations' management of their people in an effort to improve key outcomes or to otherwise improve their competitive position. The examples are organized by the major categories of outcomes to which HR analytic techniques are being applied.

EMPLOYEE ENGAGEMENT

When properly measured, increasing employee engagement can help organizations to increase employee "buy-in," to work harder, and often to produce better financial results. For example, employee engagement is tracked carefully at Best Buy, where they can identify as little as a 0.1 percent change in it.[71] Their analytics work has determined each 0.1 percent increase in engagement is associated with roughly a $100,000 increase in a store's annual gross income.

After implementing a quarterly human capital scorecard, Standard Chartered Bank found strong correlations among drivers of employee engagement and attrition at their Hong Kong branch locations.[72] The top quartile of branches with the highest levels of engagement had 46 percent lower staff attrition, and 16 percent higher profit margins, than those branches with lower engagement.

Harrah's Entertainment, which operates several casinos in Las Vegas, found through analytics that on-site health care could substantially increase their employee engagement.[73] Since implementing on-site health care, engagement has increased, turnover has decreased, and they've also saved a great deal on health care related expenses.

Marriott Vacation Club (MVC) also uses analytics to track employee engagement, gain a deeper understanding of it, and act upon those insights.[74] MVC implements changes based on employees' feedback, which has led to higher productivity within the company. They also use predictive analytics in hiring, matching sales staff candidates with the pre-determined characteristics of Marriott's top performing sales associates.

SALES

Sales is one of the most important metrics to which HR analytics techniques have been applied because of its centrality to organizational performance, straightforward measurements, and the capacity to accurately compare data across different units within an organization. For example, American Standard, which manufactures a variety of products, regularly used analytics to identify the key drivers of sales productivity across sales offices.[25] The results of the analysis identified those specific human capital practices most closely associated with the locations with the best sales results. American Standard then targeted improvement in those practices across the entire sales division, driving better results and resulting in a cycle of continuous improvement.

Corestar Financial Group, a mortgage bank company, used analytics to improve the performance of its sales staff by tracking the number of customers each employee "closed."[76] They found that some associates were far more successful at closing deals than others. As a result, the company changed its processes to route more calls to those individuals, while also working with the underperforming agents to help them improve their sales skills. This change has enabled them to grow annual sales by 45 percent, while only increasing their sales staff by 10 percent.

EMPLOYEE ABSENTEEISM

RAC, which develops advanced systems for roadside service, sought to reduce the number of days that employees missed work (regardless of the reason for the absence).[77] By conducting in-depth analysis at the office location level, they were able to find multiple location-specific solutions to employee absenteeism. As a result, they've been able to reduce the average number of sick days taken per year per employee from 10 to 8.5, which has saved the company approximately $1.5 million.

RETENTION

Employee turnover and retention of key employees is a major issue at many organizations. Ingram Content Group, a book publishing company, was dealing with a steadily increasing employee turnover rate among their distribution and fulfillment divisions, which eventually peaked at 81 percent annually across the organization (and hit 102 percent at their flagship location).[78] Intent on stemming the loss of talent, which was costly as well as highly disruptive for those employees left behind, the company used analytics to identify the primary causes of the turnover. Based on their findings, the company implemented a more selective hiring process and provided new educational, retirement and work advance programs desired by their employees. Aided by these changes, turnover fell from 81 percent to just 25 percent, saving the company $13 million dollars in the process.

The grocery store chain Wawa also used analytics to examine the reasons for their high turnover, and ended up challenging long-held assumptions in the company.[79] The company originally believed turnover was due to the large number of seasonal workers they employed (mainly high school and college students), but found that the high turnover was due more to employees' dissatisfaction about their paycheck amounts. Based on this finding, Wawa reduced the number of part-time staff members while increasing the number of full-time staff so that employees could take home more money. This resulted in a 60 percent drop in turnover over the course of four years.

INCENTIVES

Other employers have used analytics to identify the most effective motivation for their employees. Sysco, one of the largest food distributors in the United States with 161 subsidiaries, used analytics to study the way drivers were being compensated.[80] They were surprised to find that per-mile-based pay was actually a very low incentive for their drivers. Based on this finding, they began paying the drivers a base salary and incentivizing them instead for the number of deliveries made and absence of errors. As a result, several of Sysco's companies saw significant improvements in performance.

LEADERSHIP

HR analytics can help organizations to identify top-performing leaders and units, as well as the key people-related characteristics of those units and make possible a focus on those characteristics throughout the rest of the organization.

Engineering Limited, a Middle Eastern engineering firm, had been struggling to keep up with demand as they grew, promoting several leaders in the process who later proved to be ineffective, thereby creating a variety of other problems for the organization.[81] In order to minimize the possibility of similar mistakes in the future, the company used HR analytics to identify rising stars within the company and to ensure that their development focused on key skills of more successful leaders within the organization.

SAP America's North American software division had been struggling for years, routinely failing to meet key goals.[82] Recognizing the need to make a significant change, the organization turned to HR analytics, implementing a comprehensive measurement framework (see graphic below) that made it possible to link human capital processes and capabilities with key organizational results, targeting important areas of weakness.

Since implementing the process, SAP's identification and targeting of key areas has resulted in the improvement of "leadership capability" by 16 percent, as well as other related improvements in financial outcomes. Operating margin, revenue growth, capital efficiency, market share, and employee productivity have all significantly increased. "Although many developments undoubtedly contributed to the company's success, executives believe that improvements in human capital processes were an important factor in their ability to effectively execute the new strategy and, ultimately, improve financial results."[83]

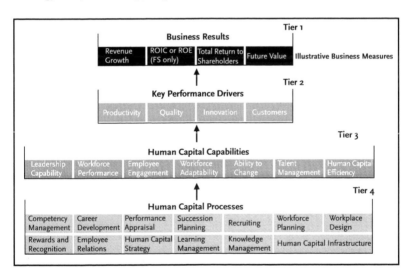

Figure 4.2 SAP's human capital development framework
Source: Susan Cantrell, James M. Benton, Terry Laudal, Robert J. Thomas, "Measuring the value of human capital investments: the SAP case," *Strategy & Leadership*, Emerald Group Publishing Limited: Vol. 34, No. 2 (2006), p. 45.

HR analytics can be used to identify key trends within a company – multiple factors that can help them grow, understand problems, identify new sources of business or even predict future outcomes based on limited information. Enterprise Rent-A-Car used the website Monster.com and its extensive database of job statistics to determine employment trends in different locations around the country in order to find the most ideal location for Enterprise's new call center.[84] They were able to identify a location with a highly educated workforce, lots of desirable candidates, and a nearby university that could provide a constant source of new hires. As a result of the careful planning and use of analytics, the new call center is now the most productive location within the company.

Major sports teams also rely heavily on analysis that is, at its core, a non-traditional form of HR analytics. One of the most prominent is the American baseball team, the Oakland A's, subject of the bestselling book *Moneyball* by Michael Lewis.[85] The Oakland franchise employed data analytics to acquire an uncharacteristic group of players, which led to multiple years of unexpected success for a team with limited financial resources. Additionally, Italian football club AC Milan uses over 60,000 data points to gauge a player's health and fitness, and ultimately to make contract decisions.

Royal Bank of Scotland Group has grown from 35,000 employees in the mid 1990's to over 135,000 employees currently.[86] To manage this substantial growth they used analytics to disseminate best practices across the organization including the best leadership traits, incentive design, recruitment, employee engagement, and business programs.

United Health Group uses predictive analytics in its recruitment efforts to track job fairs, staffing companies, and websites that have provided the longest term, most productive staff members.[87] They also developed centralized databases to break down department information "silos," streamline operations, and allow workers to have centralized access to important information and transactional data.

The Beaufort County School District (BCSD) in South Carolina sought to find new ways to improve student achievement. The district began by implementing analytics through their 27 different schools and administrative offices.[88] Measures of the human capital "maturity" across the schools (based on data collected from teachers and staff) were positively linked to measures of student outcomes (standardized test scores). The resulting analysis enabled BCSD to identify specific areas of the district's work and learning environment where the district should target its improvement efforts in order to bolster future student achievement.

Each example cited above depicts an organization confronted with a people-related question or problem, which then turned to available data and analytic techniques to identify key elements worthy of focus: whether to improve turnover, increase sales, or create incentives that lead to more productive employees.

Conclusions

5

HR analytics is a methodology and integrated process for improving the quality of decisions that have an impact or depend on people for the purpose of improving individual and/or organizational performance.

Although HR analytics is in its infancy, there is a great deal of passionate activity, writing, and research on the topic. The uses and applications of HR analytics are varied and complex. Currently, some of the most common uses include measuring and improving employee engagement, improving leadership effectiveness, and increasing sales productivity. But HR analytics has many other uses as well, such as increasing plant safety, designing effective incentives for employees to drive business results, increasing customer satisfaction, and retaining key employees.

For the most strategic types of HR analytics projects, those that link measures on the people side of the business to organizational results, a number of challenges must be addressed during the course of this work. These include identifying key performance indicators, determining the best possible analytic methods to apply to the project, effectively communicating the results, and building a follow through strategy. When considering these types of projects, it is helpful to consider where an organization might have "naturally occurring experiments" where the human drivers of key outcomes can be analyzed.

HR analytics projects also provide an authentic and meaningful way for HR professionals to be involved with key stakeholders throughout their organization, working collaboratively to help improve their most critical outcomes.

A growing body of empirical evidence indicates that the organizational benefits to HR analytics can be substantial. Organizations using HR analytics most extensively have better financial outcomes and often can cite specific examples of analytics helping to reduce costs or increase revenues. Many of these organizations also know exactly what people-related factors are driving their key business outcomes, and can intensely focus their efforts on improving those high-impact factors. Further, a growing number of case studies and other "real world" examples provide tangible evidence that HR analytics is, in fact, a realistic strategy and viable means of gaining competitive advantage.

The number of organizations that have fully integrated HR analytics into their business strategy and process as a means of achieving competitive advantage is still quite small. But as that number increases, and as the benefits of doing so become increasingly apparent, the pressure will mount for other organizations to follow suit – or risk being left behind.

Endnotes

1   John Boudreau and Peter Ramstad, *Beyond HR: The New Science of Human Capital* (Harvard Business Press, 2007) 25.

2   Jeffrey Pfeffer and Robert Sutton, *Hard Facts, Dangerous Half-Truths and Total Nonsense: Profiting from Evidence-Based Management* (Harvard Business Press, 2006).

3   Thomas Davenport, Robert Morison, and Jeanne Harris, *Analytics at Work: Smarter Decisions, Better Results* (Harvard Business Press, 2010).

4   Jac Fitz-Enz, *The New HR Analytics: Predicting the Economic Value of Your Company's Human Capital Investments* (American Management Association, 2010) 4.

5   Wayne Cascio and John Boudreau, *Investing in People: Financial Impact of Human Resource Initiatives* (FT Press, 2008) 12.

6   Pfeffer 12-13.

7   Thomas Davenport, Jeanne Harris, and Jeremy Shapiro, "Competing on Talent Analytics," *Harvard Business Review* (Oct 2010): 2-6.

8   Laurie Bassi and Daniel McMurrer, "Maximizing Your Return on People," Harvard Business Review (2007): 1-9.

9   Craig Schneider, "The New Human-Capital Metrics: A sophisticated crop of measurement tools could take the guess-work out of human-resources management," *CFO Magazine (2008): 1.*

10 Fitz-Enz 1.

11 Cascio and Boudreau 2008.

12 Davenport et al. *Competing on Talent Analytics* 4.

13 Salvatore Falletta, "HR Intelligence: Advancing People Research and Analytics," *IHRIM Journal* 12.3 (2008): 24.

14 Davenport et al. *Analytics at Work* 91.

15 Davenport et al. *Analytics at Work* 91.

16 Davenport et al. *Analytics at Work* 99-100.

17 Davenport et al. *Analytics at Work* 91.

18 Davenport et al. *Analytics at Work* 93.

19 Davenport et al. *Analytics at Work* 94.

20   Davenport et al. *Analytics at Work* 96.

21   Davenport et al. *Analytics at Work* 137

22   Mollie Lombardi, and David White, "Intelligent Human Capital Management," Aberdeen Group (2009): 6.

23   CedarCrestone, "CedarCrestone 2009-2010 HR Systems Survey," CedarCrestone (2009): 7.

24   See, e.g., CedarCrestone (2009).

25   John Gibbons and Christopher Woock, "Evidence Based Human Resources," The Conference Board (2007): 4-16.

26   Gibbons 8.

27   Laurie Bassi and Daniel McMurrer, "Does Engagement Really Drive Results?" *Talent Management Magazine* (2010):42, 43, 48.

28   Boudreau 192.

29   Philip Whiteley, "Making it count: Human capital investments that deliver improved business performance," Logica (2009): 23.

30   Whiteley 14.

31   Davenport 2-6.

32   Mollie Lombardi, and David White, "Intelligent Human Capital Management," Aberdeen Group (2009): 4-21.

33   Lombardi 6.

34   IBM-Cognos, "Getting Smart About Your Workforce," IBM-Cognos (2009): 14.

35   CedarCrestone (2009) 3.

36   IBM-Cognos 9.

37   IBM-Cognos 12.

38   Stephen Gates, "Strategic Human Capital Measures," The Conference Board (2008): 17.

39   Helen Luketic, "Human Capital Metrics Trends 2008 Survey Report," ResearchVOICE (2008): 5.

40   Mpho Magau, and Gert Roodt, "An Evaluation of the Human Capital Bridge Framework," *SA Journal of Human Resource Management* (2010): 4.

41   Magau 7-8.

42   Gates 19.

43   Gates 22.

44   IBM-Cognos 3.

45   Whiteley 18.

46   Gates 1.

47   CedarCrestone 2008 and CedarCrestone 2009.

48   We should acknowledge here that this segment of research draws heavily on articles that two of us (Bassi and McMurrer) have written. This topic – the links between specific HC

measures and business results – is a key focus of ours, and it turns out we authored a large percentage of the articles that deal with this topic.

49   Gates 8.

50   Wright et al. 2005, cited in Gates 8.

51   Lombardi 5.

52   CedarCrestone 26.

53   CedarCrestone 41.

54   Bill Roberts, "HR Analytics: Gaining Insights for the Upturn," *BusinessWeek* (2009): 1.

55   Roberts 2.

56   Laurie Bassi, and Daniel McMurrer, "Process Safety & People: Searching for the Human Capital Drivers of Process Safety," PlantSuccess.com (2008): 2.

57   Laurie Bassi, "It's All about the People: Developing and Measuring Talent at American Standard," McBassi & Company (2006): 2.

58   Bassi McMurrer, "Maximizing Your Return on People," 3.

59   Bassi "It's All about the People," 8.

60   Bassi "Maximizing Your Return on People," 5.

61   Susan Cantrell, James Benton, Terry Laudal, and Robert Thomas, "Measuring the value of human capital investments," *Strategy and Leadership* 34.2 (2006): 50.

62   Cantrell 50.

63   Gates 26.

64   Bassi "Maximizing Your Return on People," 6.

65   Laurie Bassi and Daniel McMurrer, "Human Capital Benchmarking in Further Education Preliminary Findings," Department for Education and Skills (2006):14.

66   Kate Feather, "Helping HR to measure up," *Strategic HR Review* 7.1 (2008): 28.

67   Bassi "Maximizing Your Return on People," 6.

68   Laurie Bassi and Daniel McMurrer. "Human Capital Management Predicts Stock Prices," McBassi & Company, (2010): 1-2.

69   Laurie Bassi and Daniel McMurrer, "Toward a Human Capital Measurement Methodology," *Advances in Developing Human Resources* 10.6 (2008): 872.

70   Bassi "Toward a Human Capital Measurement Methodology," 14.

71   Davenport et al. "Competing on Talent Analytics" 4.

72   Whiteley 28.

73   Davenport et al. "Competing on Talent Analytics" 3.

74   Gates 24.
75   Bassi "It's All about the People," 13.
76   Craig Schneider, "The New Human-Capital Metrics: A sophis-
      ticated crop of measurement tools could take the guesswork out of
      human-resources management," *CFO Magazine (2008): 2.*
77   IBM-Cognos, "A seat at the table," IBM-Cognos (2009): 11.
78   Fitz-Enz 217.
79   Roberts 1.
80   Schneider 3.
81   Fitz-Enz 240.
82   Cantrell 7.
83   Cantrell 49.
84   Fitz-Enz 224.
85   Davenport et al. "Competing on Talent Analytics" 4.
86   Gates 13.
87   Fitz-Enz 265.
88   Bassi "Human Capital Benchmarking in Further Education," 4.
89   Given the explosion of writing in this area and the sheer
      breadth of the field, there were almost certainly some works
      that were not included in this initial collection; please notify
      the authors if you're aware of a work that you would suggest
      considering for review in future reports.

Appendices

Appendix A

Over the past two years, our colleagues at iNostix set about gathering all recent articles, reports, and books that they could locate on the topic of HR analytics.[89] In order to maximize the timeliness of this report, we limited our review to only material written in 2006 or later. This included over 80 works.

We ranked each article and report based on the criteria listed in the table on the following page. Each was ranked by two of the three authors of this report, with the rankings then compared and any discrepancies resolved through further review. (We did not apply this ranking method to books considered for inclusion.)

We selected for inclusion in this handbook all works that were classified as category 1, 2, 3a, 3b, or 3c. The others, which included many valuable documents as well, were excluded due to their relative lack of empirical data, which represents the primary focus of this handbook. Each article or report in these categories was then broken down in detail, with a separate "technical summary" of each document prepared as a foundation for the writing of this handbook.

Table A-1 List of categories for selecting and reviewing documents for inclusion.

Category 1	Analyzes impact of actual human capital measures (e.g., specific leadership or learning practices) on HARD business outcomes (revenue per employee, turnover rates, etc.)
Category 2	Analyzes impact of actual human capital measures (e.g., specific leadership or learning practices) on SOFT business outcomes (self-reported profitability vs. peers, "better", "same", "worse", etc.)
Category 3a	Includes data on use of HR analytics or applications (talent management systems, etc.) and analyzes the impact of the use of those measurement methods on organizational outcomes (hard or soft).
Category 3b	No analysis of any impact on outcomes, but includes other actual data related to use of HR analytics, typically survey results on extent of use of various types of analytic methods.
Category 3c	No analysis of any impact on outcomes, but discusses survey results on extent of use of various types of analytic methods, includes no data.
Category 4	Presents developed conceptual framework on ways in which HR analytics should be deployed and/or incorporated into business operations.
Category 5a	No analysis, but includes specific "how-to's" about ways to start using HR analytics within an organization.
Category 5b	Makes the case that HR analytic methods should be used, but without any analysis/hard evidence, no how-to's or framework.

Appendix B

DOCUMENTS USED

Aberdeen Group. "HRX 2.0™: The Next Generation of HR Executives." Aberdeen Group. April 2009.

Bassi, Laurie. "It's All About the People: Developing and Measuring Talent at American Standard." *mcbassi.com. May 2006. Web 10 October 2010.* <http://www.mcbassi.com/resources/documents/AmericanStandard.pdf>.

Bassi, Laurie and Daniel McMurrer. "Human Capital Management Predicts Stock Prices." mcbassi.com. June 2010. Web 23 October 2010. <http://mcbassi.com/documents/HCMPredictsStockPrices.pdf>.

Bassi, Laurie and Daniel McMurrer. "Does Engagement Really Drive Results?" *Talent Management Magazine* (March 2010): 42-48. < http://www.mcbassi.com/documents/HCMPredictsStockPrices.pdf>.

Bassi, Laurie and Daniel McMurrer. "Process Safety & People: Searching for the Human Capital Drivers of Process Safety." *plantsuccess*.com. 2008. Web 10 October 2010. <http://www.mcbassi.net/resources/documents/PlantSuccessWhitePaper.pdf>.

Bassi, Laurie and Daniel McMurrer. "Toward a Human Capital Measurement Methodology." *Advances in Developing Human Resources* 10.6 (2008): 2-19.

Bassi, Laurie and Daniel McMurrer. "Maximizing Your Return on People." *Harvard Business Review.* (March 2007): 1-9.

Bassi, Laurie and Daniel McMurrer. "Beyond Employee Satisfaction, ROI, and the Balanced Score Card: Improving Business Results Through Improved Human Capital Measurement." *The 2006 Pfeiffer Annual: Human Resource Management.* 2006. 3-15.

Bassi, Laurie and Daniel McMurrer. "Human Capital Benchmarking in Further Education: Preliminary Findings." *U.K. Department for Education and Skills.* Ref# RW88. 2006.

Birkman International. "HR Measurement and Metrics: Gaining HR a Seat at the Strategy Table." *Birkman International.* 2008.

Blyth, Alex. "HR metrics help HR to prove its worth." *Personneltoday. com.* 09 October. 2008. Web 10 October 2010.

Boudreau, John and Peter Ramstad. *Beyond HR: The New Science of Human Capital.* Boston. Harvard Business Press. 2007.

BusinessWeek. "HR Innovation: Make Fact-based Talent Decisions with Workforce Analytics." *BusinessWeek.* (February 2008): 4-11.

Cascio, Wayne and John Boudreau. *Investing in People: Financial Impact of Human Resource Initiatives.* New Jersey. FT Press. 2008.

Cantrell, Susan and James Benton, and Terry Laudal, and Robert Thomas. "Measuring the value of human capital investments: the SAP case." *Strategy & Leadership.* 34.2 (2006): 1-10.

CedarCrestone. "CedarCrestone 2009-2010 HR Systems Survey: HR Technologies, Deployment Approaches, Value and Metrics." CedarCrestone. 2009.

CedarCrestone. "CedarCrestone 2008-2009 HR Systems Survey: HR Technologies, Service Delivery Approaches, and Metrics." CedarCrestone. 2008.

CedarCrestone. "CedarCrestone Metrics & Analytics: 2008 HR Systems Mid-year Survey Update." CedarCrestone. 2008.

CedarCrestone. "CedarCrestone 2007 Metrics and Analytics Report: A Supplement to the Ninth Annual Edition of the CedarCrestone HCM Survey." CedarCrestone. 2007.

Davenport, Thomas, Jeanne Harris, and Jeremy Shapiro. "Competing on Talent Analytics." *Harvard Business Review.* (October 2010): 2-6.

Davenport, Thomas, Robert Morison, and Jeanne Harris. *Analytics at Work: Smarter Decisions, Better Results.* Boston. Harvard Business Press. 2010.

Falletta, Salvatore. "HR Intelligence: Advancing People Research and Analytics." *IHRIM Journal* 12.3 (2008): 21-31.

Feather, Kate. "Helping HR to measure up: arming the "soft" function with hard metrics." *Strategic HR Review* 7.1 (2008): 1-5.

Fitz-Enz, Jac. *The New HR Analytics: Predicting the Economic Value of Your Company's Human Capital Investments.* New York: American Management Association, 2010.

Gates, Stephen. "Strategic Human Capital Measures: Orientation, Accountability, and Communication." *The Conference Board*. Ref# R-1417-08-WG. 2008.

Gibbons, John and Christopher Woock. "Evidence-Based Human Resources: A Primer and Summary of Current Literature." *The Conference Board*. Ref# E-0015-07-RR. 2007.

Harris, Jeanne, Elizabeth Craig, and Henry Egan. "How to Create a Talent-Powered Analytical Organization." Accenture Institute for High Performance. 2009.

IBM-Cognos. "A seat at the table: How smart HR departments win with business intelligence." IBM-Cognos. 2009.

IBM-Cognos. "Getting Smart About Your Workforce: Why Analytics Matter." IBM-Cognos. 2009.

Lockwood, Nancy. "Maximizing Human Capital: Demonstrating HR Value With Key Performance Indicators." *Society for Human Resource Management*. 2006.

Lombardi, Mollie and David White. "Intelligent Human Capital Management: Workforce Analytics Drives Profit and Performance." Aberdeen Group. 2009.

Luketic, Helen. "Human Capital Metrics Trends 2008: Survey Report." *ResearchVOICE*. (2008): 3-17.

Magau, M.D, & G Roodt. (2010). "An evaluation of the Human Capital BRidge™ framework." *SA Journal of Human Resource Management/ SA Tydskrifvir Menslikehulpbronsbestuur*, 8(1), Art. #276.

Peiseniece, Liga and Tatjana Volkova. "Necessity to Evaluate Human Resource Management in Companies of Latvia." *Economics and Management*. 15 (2010): 698-704.

Pfeffer, Jeffrey and Robert Sutton. *Hard Facts, Dangerous Half-Truths and Total Nonsense: Profiting from Evidence-Based Management*. Boston. Harvard Business Press. 2006.

Roberts, Bill. "HR Analytics: Gaining Insights for the Upturn." *Business Week*. (May 2009): 1-4.

Schneider, Craig. "The New Human-Capital Metrics: A sophisticated crop of measurement tools could take the guesswork out of human-resources management." *CFO Magazine*. (Feb 2008): 1-5.

Scott-Jackson, William, Petra Cook, and Randal Tajer. "Measures of workforce capability for future performance: Identifying the measures that matter most." *Chartered Management Institute*. 2008.

SHRM. "SHRM® Human Capital Benchmarking Study: 2008 Executive Summary." *Society for Human Resource Management*. 2008.

Taleo Research. "Measure, Report, Analyze, and Improve: Turning Analytics into Action." *Taleo Research*. 2006.

Tootell, Beth, Meredith Blackler, Paul Toulson, and Philip Dewe. "Metrics: HRM's Holy Grail? A New Zealand Case Study." *Human Resource Management Journal 19.4* (2009): 375-92.

Vance, David. *The Business of Learning*. Poudre River Press. 2010.

Whiteley, Philip. "Making it Count: Human Capital Investments that deliver improved business performance." Logica. 2009.

Baker, Stephen. "Data Mining Moves to Human Resources." *Predictive Analytics*. March 2009.

Barrett, Mary. "Metrics: Do They Matter Anymore or Do They Matter More?" Association of American Medical Colleges. March 2010.

Bassi, Laurie and Daniel McMurrer. "Human Capital Analytics: Aligning People and Results." mcbassi.com. McBassi & Company. 2009.

Boudreau, John. "HR measures that drive strategic decisions: optimizing decisions about talent." *IBM: Innovation in Action Series. (*May 2009): 2-11.

Boudreau, John and Peter Ramstad. "Talentship and HR Measurement and Analysis: From ROI to Strategic Organizational Change." *Human Resource Planning*. (2006): 25-33.

Briner, Rob. "Is HRM evidence-based and does it matter?" Integrated Employer Solutions. 2007.

Brown, Andy and Steve Kelly. "Connecting staff research with company success: a practical guide to developing an effective measurement program." Melcrum Publishing, Ltd. (2006): 24-27.

Butterfield, Barbara. "Powerful Metrics: Strategic and Transformative." *CUPA-HR Journal* 57.2 (2006): 4-11.

Chhinzer, Nita and Gurdeep Ghatehorde. "Challenging Relationships: HR Metrics and Organizational Financial Performance." *The Journal of Business Inquiry* 8.1 (2009): 37-48.

Corporate Executive Board. "Improving HR Business Partner Effectiveness." Corporate Executive Board. 2007.

Davenport, Thomas. "Competing on Analytics." *Harvard Business Review*. Ref# R0601H. 2005.

DiBernardino, Frank and Adrianne Miller. "Human Capital Analytics – The Missing Link: Measuring Financial Returns on the Human Capital Investment." Vienna Human Capital Advisors. 2008.

Fitz-Enz, Jac. "Predicting People: From Metrics to Analytics." *Wiley Periodicals, Inc.* (2009): 1-10.

Fitz-Enz, Jac. "Predictive Management: How to Optimize Human Capital." *Human Capital Source*. (2008): 2-8.

Fitz-Enz, Jac. "Beyond Benchmarking: Value-Adding Metrics." *CUPA-HR Journal* 58.2 (2007): 12-16.

Hansen, Fay. "Special Report: The HR Profession-HR at America's Most Admired Companies." *Workforce Management.* (June 2008): 24-32.

HR Focus. "Benchmarking for Functional HR Metrics." *HR Focus* 83.11 (2006): 1, 13-15.

IBM-Cognos. "Metrics and Dimensions in IBM Cognos 8 Workforce Performance." IBM-Cognos. 2009.

IBM. "Aligning your people with business strategy using workforce analytics." IBM Global Business Services. 2008.

Kelly, Jeff. "Human resources data analytics bring metrics to workforce management." SearchBusinessAnalytics.com. December 2008.

McLean, Gary. "Examining approaches to HR evaluation: The strengths and weaknesses of popular measurement methods." Melcrum Publishing ltd 4.2 (2005): 24-27.

Phillips, Jack and Patricia Phillips. "Measuring return on investment in HR." *Strategic HR Review* 8.6 (2009): 12-19.

Phillips, Jack and Patricia Phillips. *Show Me the Money: How to Determine ROI in People, Projects, and Programs.* Berrett-Koehler Publishers, Inc. 2007.

Robinson, Dilys. "Human capital measurement: an approach that works." *Strategic HR Review* 8.6 (2009): 5-11.

SAS. "Predictive Performance Management." SAS Institute, Inc. 2009.

SAS. "The Aligned Organization: How performance management can align activities and resources with enterprise level strategy and market conditions." SAS Institute, Inc. 2008.

SAS. "Aligned Resource Optimization: How to optimally allocate resources in alignment with enterprise-level objectives." SAS Institute, Inc. 2008.

SAS. "The HR Imperative for Predictive Modeling: Elevate recruitment and retention to strategic status with advanced analytics." SAS Institute, Inc. 2007.

SAS. "From Tactical to Strategic: Redefining the Role of the Chief Human Capital Officer." SAS Institute. 2007.

Schwarz, Joshua and Thomas Murphy. "Human Capital Metrics: An Approach to Teaching Using Data and Metrics to Design and Evaluate Management Practices." *Journal of Management Education* 32. (2007): 164-80.

Shapiro, Jeremy. "Benchmarking the Benchmarks." *HR Magazine* 55.4 (2010): 1-5.

Shapiro, Jeremy. "How to 'Make Over' Your HR Metrics." *HR Focus*. (September 2007): 3-4.

Sturman, Michael. "Helping HR to measure up: arming the "soft" function with hard metrics." *Strategic HR Review* 7.1 (2008): 1-5.

Vaillancourt, Allison. "Here's the Answer: Was There a Question? Avoiding the top 10 Metrics Mistakes." *CUPA-HR Journal* 58.2 (2007): 2, 6-10.

Ventana Research. "Workforce Analytics and Business Intelligence: Understanding and Improving Workforce Performance." Ventana Research. 2008.

Whitaker, Debbie. "Human Capital: Management or Measurement." *Personnel Today Magazine*. February 2007.

Dr. Laurie Bassi
is the CEO and a co-founder of
McBassi & Company. She is
one of the world's leading
authorities on human capital
analytics.

Rob Carpenter
is a project manager at
McBassi, where he has
key responsibilities for
client projects, business
development, and small
business consulting.

Dan McMurrer
is the chief analyst and a
co-founder of McBassi &
Company, where he oversees
McBassi's project management
and on-going research
initiatives.

McBassi & Company takes the guesswork out of the "people side" of your business. McBassi offers a variety of tools to deliver actionable business intelligence, including the pioneering McBassi People Index® framework, a research-based employee questionnaire; customized analysis services; and HR analytics workshops for your organization.

McBassi identifies the unique human drivers of your organization's results and points the way to sustainable competitive advantage.

ABOUT THE RESEARCHERS

Luk Smeyers and **Jeroen Delmotte** gathered the research summarized in this handbook. Both are owners of Europe's HR Analytics Expertise Bureau iNostix.